Matters of the Heart & Soul

Matters of the Heart & Soul

Encouraging Insights on the Human Journey

John J. Montalvo

iUniverse, Inc.

New York   Bloomington

MATTERS OF THE HEART & SOUL
Encouraging Insights on the Human Journey
Copyright © 2008 by John J. Montalvo

iUniverse books may be ordered through booksellers or by contacting:

iUniverse
1663 Liberty Drive
Bloomington, IN 47403
www.iuniverse.com
1-800-Authors (1-800-288-4677)

ISBN: 978-0-595-46419-7 (pbk)
ISBN: 978-1-4401-0338-4 (cloth)
ISBN: 978-0-595-90713-7 (ebk)

Library of Congress Control Number: 2009901257

Printed in the United States of America

iUniverse rev. date: 03/04/2009

I dedicate this book to my parents, John and Elizabeth, whom I love more than words can express.

Author's note: Some themes and categories in this book overlap from one chapter to another due to their wide applications.

Contents

Acknowledgments

MY ETERNAL GRATITUDE TO:

My parents, John Montalvo and Elizabeth Plaza-Smith, for their generous and unceasing loving support that enabled me to achieve many of my lifelong dreams.

My amazing girlfriend, Jenny Ramirez, for her illuminating kindness and her complete belief in my book, from its conception to its realization.

My late grandmother, Celia López-Montalvo, for teaching me at a young age that any noble endeavor is worthwhile and indeed possible.

My sister, Kim Montalvo, for her persistent faith and bravery during her battle with cancer and kidney failure. Her determination to remain positive and to soldier-on was an inspiration to us all.

My younger brother, Neal Kenneth Smith, whose friendly, outgoing nature and infectious laughter make it a true honor and joy to know him; I am proud to call him brother.

Our family's eternal hero, Daniel Caruso (Kim's kidney donor), for his noble sacrifice and selfless humanity. His generosity will never be forgotten.

Barbara Johnson, a wonderful person and humanitarian, for offering her professional writing experience and time in this freshman endeavor.

All those, past and present, whose eloquent and indelible insights have added to the foundation of this book.

My most dear relatives and longtime friends, for their steadfast devotion and their much-needed prayers during trying times.

And those who lead the many to righteousness, like the stars forever and ever. (Dan. 12:3 NASB)

Introduction

Every human being has the potential to expand his horizons—to reach higher in life. Though, as many I'm sure will agree, we can always benefit from a few timely words of encouragement, to further inspire us to attain our goals.

Matters of the Heart & Soul is a collection of personal writings and insightful works that I have put together over the span of many years. It is a book about personal growth, introspection, and self-discovery. It is also a motivational piece written and carefully edited for a reflective and soul-searching audience. Ultimately, its main objective is to encourage readers to think about life a little differently—to challenge their intellect and give them a more meaningful perspective on themselves and the world around them.

In addition to my personal reflections and musings on everyday life issues, *Matters of the Heart & Soul* will also provide you with some time-honored wisdom from the *Holy Bible*, along with many fitting and memorable quotes from prominent personalities and world luminaries, past and present including Ralph Waldo Emerson, Albert Einstein, Helen Keller, Martin Luther King, Jr., and Billy Graham. With these and other esteemed figures' life perspectives, this book will serve to inspire and uplift the reader to new, greater heights.

Another purpose of this book is to share with others the important virtues and ideals that I have learned during the course of my life.

My simple philosophy (though hardly original) has long been to take whatever situation life hands me—good or bad—to strive to make it better, moreover, to turn temporary failure into meaningful success. For many years a significant part of my writings, based on my strong beliefs in the power of prayer, faith, and positive thinking, have enabled me to do this—and I believe that they can do the same for others.

All in all, *Matters of the Heart & Soul* is about the deeper issues that matter most in life, with a particular emphasis on enduring peace, love, friendship, universal truths, freedom, family values, and unity. It's about how all these are inextricably linked, and how these common core beliefs inherently connect us all, for the greater good. I hope that the words in this book will have a positive impact on your life and give you additional inspiration and guidance on your intrepid journey.

Chapter One: The Human Journey

To venture causes anxiety, but not to venture is to lose one's self ... and to venture in the highest sense is precisely to become conscious of one's self.
—Søren Kierkegaard

Ω

The following is a fitting sentiment that I came across during my personal research on book publishing. Its practical message continues to be a source of inspiration for me. My wish for you is that the many similar, insightful themes throughout my book will inspire you in the same manner, and bring you closer to realizing your special hopes and dreams.

Ω

It is not ease but effort, not facility but difficulty that makes a man. There is perhaps no station in life in which difficulties do not have to be encountered and overcome before any decided means of success can be achieved.

—Samuel Smiles, Scottish author

Waiting to Be Known

Just as there is an infinite number of luminous stars in the universe, there is an infinite number of illuminating ideas ... waiting to be known, explored and shared.

Ω

The Mind Knows no Limits

There are many frontiers waiting for us over the horizon, as there are in an uncharted wilderness and distant heavenly worlds. Yet despite their exceeding numbers and vast distances, they are all reachable ... in the imaginative, unrelenting human mind.

Ω

A Special Art

Vision is the talent of making the invisible visible to all.

Ω

Among the Stars

In the course of our journey through life, we will experience many unexpected roadblocks and detours, due mostly to circumstances beyond our control. However, we must not be discouraged, but continue to diligently stay the course, not allowing anything nor anyone to prevent us from completing our life's obligation ... from discovering who we really are and what our incredible human purpose is among the glowing stars.

Time Is of the Essence

Today is yesterday's future and the present is tomorrow's past. That's how short life is—that's how long we have. Let us redeem any loss of time by pressing forward. Together, with open minds and brave hearts, let us begin the wondrous journey.

Ω

For this is the journey that men make to find themselves.

—James Michener, *The Fires of Spring*

Ω

Coming into My Own

Early in my life, I sensed something moving—something happening in and around me, day after day, growing. Then suddenly, one day, it became very clear; I understood the meaning; I was growing up and becoming my own person ... becoming my own man.

Ω

I Am

I am what you see. I can't explain how I became, but just the same, I am who I am, and in this world I came to be me.

Ω

Being Real

I may not always know what I want in life; I may not always know what I feel. But one thing I will always know is that I need to be real when I feel what I feel.

On Personal Growth

In critical decision making, trust not in your heart at first, but in that which you already know to be sound and true. Making rationally balanced decisions, based on life experiences, is a clear sign of one's maturity.

Ω

Maturity

Maturity means personal growth—knowing what is right and doing it, despite what others may think of you.

Ω

Keep away from people who try to belittle your ambitions. Small people always do that, but the really great ones make you feel that you too, can become great.

—Mark Twain, writer and humorist

Ω

Bold Minds Think Alike

I remember one day in my youth saying the following words to myself, not knowing at the time that writer Emile Zola (1840-1902) had also said the exact thing more than a century ago. All the same, the bold expression holds true for me still: "I am here to live out loud."

Ω

The bravest are surely those who have the clearest vision of what is before them, glory and danger alike, and yet notwithstanding go out to meet it.

—Thucydides, Greek historian

Being Who I Am

Certain times in my life I've had the displeasure of interacting with strange personality-types, who, for whatever reason, presumptuously went out of their way to try to change me into something I was not—something, according to their mindset or estimation, "better" or "higher" than my true self. Instead of taking their insincere efforts to heart and listening to those whose true motive was only to belittle me, I just went on living as I always have, being who I am ... being all of me.

Ω

Why?

Tell me, if I can't be me, then why is it I am who I am?

Ω

On Pretentiousness

Being pretentious will never produce satisfying relationships ... just contention and loneliness. It is a waste of effort and precious time.

Ω

Your True Self

Being "you" simply means being true to yourself while also growing as a human being ... and knowing what you want to be.

Ω

At the heart of your being lies your answer. You know who you are and what you want.

—Laozi, Chinese philosopher

Exploring Your Potential

People will tell you "Everything will be fine if you just be yourself." Sometimes I don't want to just "be myself," accept the status quo, and be content with that. What I want in life is to excel, to do all I can to better myself—to maximize my potential. For me, the simple notion of being oneself—to the point of dull complacency—is not enough. If I am to exceed my wildest dreams, I must "throw off the bowlines," venture outward with raised sails, and explore uncharted worlds.

Ω

Make It So

Avoid contemptuous souls who take pleasure in mocking your dreams. If you cannot avoid them, then turn their jeers into cheers by making your noble dreams come true.

Ω

The world makes way for the man who knows where he is going.

—Ralph Waldo Emerson, essayist and poet

Chapter Two: Perspectives on Success

To win without risk is to triumph without glory.

—Pierre Corneille

Ω

In a Free World

Freedom is the opportunity to take action, to take your hopes and cherished dreams and turn them into a shining reality. In a free world, a noble dream is more than a possibility.

Ω

Getting Back to the Basics

Here I am today, wondering if I am doing what I should be doing to further my aspirations in life, or if I am allowing myself to become complacent. Regardless of the answer, to fulfill my dreams and achieve my goals, I must be more diligent, as the saying goes, "There is no room for compromise, only room for improvement."

Whatever is worth doing at all is worth doing well.

—Philip Dormer Stanhope, Earl of Chesterfield

Ω

Determination may open doors for you, but only ability and unfailing resolve will keep them open.

Ω

When you set out to accomplish a job and when time is of the essence, be bold; make your own intelligent shortcuts, instead of wasting precious time looking for them.

Ω

Four words that stand between you and your dream: *I can't do it.*

Ω

A setback remains a setback until one makes a *comeback.*

Ω

Hard work becomes less hard the harder you work.

Ω

Think like a man of passion. Act like a man of principle.

At Its Best

The striving for personal perfection, knowing that it won't fully be attained, is human nature at its best.

Ω

Self-Pity

Self-pity is my worst enemy. When feeling sorry for myself, I accomplish nothing.

Ω

The True Warrior

Sometimes we are our own worst enemy, in matters large and small. But he who can conquer his reckless and wayward self, and rule his own destiny, is the greatest warrior of them all.

Ω

A Good Thing

If you want to do a good thing in life, start simply by taking good care of your own—that is to say, stop doubting yourself and start believing in your inherent gifts and talents, and in due time, peace of mind and self-confidence will abound in your precious soul.

Ω

Get to It

To the slothful man, I assert that, if you do not see to your responsibilities, nothing will ever get done. Arise now; awake from your slumber with diligent hands and finish what you have begun.

Contrary to the cynic's point of view, all good dreams do come true.

$$\Omega$$

The Straight and Narrow

As I look ahead towards the straight and narrow road, I can see a great destiny in the making. One filled with honor, dignity, and glory. A destiny that is not only achievable but indeed also worthy of any personal sacrifice. What lies at the end is eternal joy in paradise.

$$\Omega$$

[F]orgetting those things which are behind and reaching forward to those things which are ahead, I press toward the goal for the prize of the upward call of God in Christ Jesus. (Phil. 3:13–14)

$$\Omega$$

True Values

In the world we have the seemingly rich (the Haves) and the poor (the Have-nots). It seems neither one can subsist without the other. I, however, am convinced that anyone can become exceedingly rich in the world by simply choosing the right values in life, the ones that lead to personal integrity, real happiness, and prosperity.

$$\Omega$$

Patience

Patience leads to fulfillment and rewards; hard work guarantees it.

The Ultimate Reward

One can say that a goal in life can be compared to a fine object made of pure gold—precious in value, pleasing to the eye, and once attained, more intoxicating than vintage wine.

Ω

Life is either a daring adventure or nothing. Security does not exist in nature, nor do the children of men as a whole experience it. Avoiding danger is no safer in the long run than outright exposure.

—Helen Keller, writer and lecturer

Ω

Staying Positive

Three words that propel you to meet bold challenges and overcome great obstacles: *Yes, I can.*

Ω

Pursuing the Goal

Today I have found a new purpose for my life—another inspiring goal, a goal I strongly believe to be worthy of my interest, one I plan to pursue with vigor and determination. I will hold onto it until I see it to fruition, until I become as one with its empowering light.

Ω

Arriving at one goal is the starting point to another.

—John Dewey, philosopher

A musician must make music, an artist must paint, a poet must write, if he is ultimately to be at peace with himself.

—Abraham Maslow, psychologist

Ω

The Right Plan

In life we are presented with many goal-opportunities—with diverse career options to choose from. We must look closely to assess the right goal to pursue. When you make your decision, be ready to devise an intelligent plan for success and to face expected and unexpected challenges. Failure to plan wisely will delay your success.

Ω

Make It Happen

Find a meaningful goal to pursue in life. If you can't find one, create one. It's that simple.

Ω

The Challenge

One of the biggest challenges in life is to remain persistent in what you do, even when boredom sets in. This is a true mark of character: persistence leads to perseverance.

Ω

A Small Reminder

It is better to try and later cry than to cry for not having tried at all.

Journalist Sydney J. Harris once stated, "Regret for the things we did can be tempered by time; it is regret for the things we did not do that is inconsolable."

Ω

A Winning Attitude

One day I asked myself, "What can be more important than winning?" Then a little voice inside me said, "Nothing, except in knowing that by giving your all, and doing your best, you don't always have to win to be a winner."

Ω

Precious Dreams

You are free to dream, so when you do, use the gift of imagination and dream big. It would be wisest to do so with both feet planted firmly on the ground, and, with steadfast effort, you will achieve your precious dreams by leaps and bounds.

Ω

To Believe

To dream is to believe; to believe is to see your dreams already fulfilled.

Ω

They who dream by day are cognizant of many things which escape those who dream only by night.

—Edgar Allan Poe, writer

U.S. president and Nobel Prize winner Woodrow Wilson said we grow great by dreams. "All big men are dreamers. They see things in the soft haze of a spring day or in the red fire of a long winter's evening. Some of us let these great dreams die but others nourish and protect them, nurse them through bad days 'til they bring them to the sunshine and light' which comes always to those who sincerely hope that their dreams will come true."

Ω

Let There Be Vision

Let there be vision. Where there is vision, even the meaning of the word "nothing" can give rise to something, for even out of nothing, something good can flourish—a new and wondrous beginning. Did not the miracle of the earth and the universe begin this way?

Ω

The earth was without form, and void; and darkness was on the face of the deep ... Then God said, "Let there be light," and there was light. And God saw the light, that it was good. (Gen. 1:2–4)

Ω

The greatest tragedy in life is people who have sight but no vision.

—Helen Keller, writer and lecturer

Ω

Nothing Ventured, Nothing Gained

Success is not some acquired thing that one can obtain without concentrated effort. Despite what anyone says, success still requires persistent blood, sweat, and tears ... not to mention, courage.

Simple Devices

We are constantly bombarded on television and radio with infomercials that offer (at an affordable price) guaranteed keys to success. But as most sensible people already know, keys, in general, have nothing to do with real success; they are merely devices whose sole function is to operate machines, nothing more.

Ω

When Opportunity Knocks

When opportunity knocks, don't waste precious time asking, "Who is it?" for it is better to just open the door widely and embrace "it" with open arms, as you would a trusted friend.

Ω

Successful Living

There are no specialized keys to success, or secret formulas. The secret to success is no secret at all: success—that is successful living—is just a matter of applying certain principles in our daily lives, such as commitment, drive, dedication, and perseverance.

Ω

Failure is not fatal. Only failure to get back up is.

—John C. Maxwell, author

Ω

Making It to the Top

Making it to the top is not the hardest job; it's staying there. Success is fleeting if you don't work diligently to maintain it.

There are only 3 colors, 10 digits, and 7 notes; it's what we do with them that's important.

—Ruth Ross

Ω

Savoring the Climb

Achieving success is like reaching a wonderful orgasm of the mind. But if it comes too fast and easy, the gratification is short-lived.

Ω

Earning It

Gaining self-esteem is much like gaining respect: before it can be obtained, it first must be earned.

Ω

Conquering Mondays

We all know that Monday is the hardest day of the week, but we must get by Monday in order to contend with Tuesday.

Ω

Facing Adversity

Each day we face in life is like a cosmic game of chess, a game of strategy and sacrifice. We move and countermove like warriors in contemplation of victory; we advance onward with caution, and to regroup, wisely pull back. In the end, ultimate victory will be ours if we remain morally calm and steadfast in the face of existing and looming adversity.

The Interview

Interviewer: In your book you write philosophically on many facets of the human condition, such as love, war, hate, peace, family unity, spirituality, success, etc. In so many words, how would you best describe life's basic meaning and what advice would you give to someone who is just starting out with hopes of finding success?

J J M: Plain and simple, life's a struggle—an ongoing uphill struggle. It is the ultimate battle of attrition—and the sooner all come to accept this cosmic truth, the better chance for lasting success we will all have.

Ω

A Positive Outlook

If I were to define success, it would be this: success is looking back with a smile while looking forward to tomorrow; success is appreciating every day.

Ω

The Sky's the Limit

My true success in life lies in part in my unwillingness to listen to the self-doubting voices from within, and not giving up my quest of reaching for the sky.

Ω

For the Time Being

Learn to be content with less for the time being, for this will mean a lot. But strive for more no matter what; hold on to your precious dreams.

Avoiding Boredom

Contrary to popular perception, smart people do not get bored so easily for the simple reason that they're too busy engaging themselves in myriad pursuits that further challenge their able bodies, wondrous minds, and adventurous souls.

Ω

Being bored is an insult to oneself.

—Jules Renard, writer

Ω

Something to Think About

There's a big difference between intelligent people and smart people. Intelligent people have much knowledge; smart people utilize it.

Ω

Honing One's Skills

Inspirational words can spark one's creative will, but a great poem or sentiment alone cannot and will not build a great future city, nor an ultramodern community. In building a better world for tomorrow, we need both inspiration and know-how.

Ω

A Purposeful Life

A purposeful life is about goal-setting—applying effort to one's dreams and aspirations. Without these, there can be no gratifying sense of accomplishment nor higher sense of human achievement.

Chapter Three: Life's Gifts
(Happiness, Friendship, Love and Spirituality)

The happiest of people don't necessarily have the best of everything; they just make the most of everything that comes along their way.

—Author unknown

Ω

A State of Mind

In all my experiences I've come to find that happiness is displaying a positive mental attitude in all circumstances. Happiness is a state of mind, and one I will do my extreme best to remain in. As Abraham Lincoln said, "People are about as happy as they make up their minds to be."

Ω

Honor First

Happiness is a virtual impossibility without honor and integrity. A lack of self-honor equals self-misery.

There can be no happiness if the things we believe in are different from the things we do.

—Freya Madeline Stark, traveler and writer

Ω

Complete Trust

Knowing who your friends are makes you the happiest man in the world. Knowing whom you can trust in life says it all.

Ω

Value your Friends

Life is empty without a friend—a lonely existence. Think about this before you tell a good friend, "Leave me alone."

Ω

On Friendship

When it comes to friendship, openness is not enough; what brings us together is closeness and love.

Ω

There is no better mirror than an old friend.

—Japanese proverb

Here to Stay

The saying "Friends come and go" is not true. Acquaintances come and go; real friends never leave you, for wherever they are, there you will be, and wherever you are, there they will be.

Ω

It Takes Time

Like all good and wonderful things in life, it takes time for friendship to grow. It takes dedicated nurturing and continual trust.

Ω

Sole Motive

This is the making of a true friend: a person whose only motive is to aspire to be true to you at all times.

Ω

Tell me who your friends are, and I will tell you who you are.

—Ancient Assyrian proverb

A True Friend

True friends are those who show their affection for you without hesitation and, in your moments of personal triumph or defeat, count it a special honor to stand by your side.

Ω

Truer words on the value of a loyal friend were never spoken than those said by Greek playwright Euripides: "One loyal friend is worth ten thousand relatives."

Friend or Foe

The stronger we develop our friendships with existing allies, the stronger our resolve will be against any present or potential foe.

Ω

The More the Better

It is better to have more friends than mere acquaintances. The more friends we have, the more we have to live for.

Ω

We cannot really love anybody with whom we never laugh.

—Agnes Repplier, American essayist

Ω

To Be Liked

In order to be liked, one has to be loving. In order to be loved, one should radiate happiness when giving. Love can only be assured if you are willing.

Ω

Kindred Souls

The unceasing, binding love between kindred souls is stronger than all the negative forces that conspire to oppose it. Envious, hostile forces won't stand a chance against its undying loyalty.

The Ultimate Price

The ultimate price for a committed loving relationship is complete selflessness on both sides.

Ω

Be Proactive

A practical explanation for love: love is proactive, not inactive.

Ω

Authentic love is not a vague sentiment or a blind passion. It is an inner attitude that involves the whole human being. Love, in a word, is the gift of self.

—Pope John Paul II

Ω

Get Moving

Love has no time to think. When urgently needed, it responds immediately.

Ω

A Strategy for Love

If you feel like you are not being loved enough, then get busy loving others that much more, for the busier you are giving your love to others, the less time you will have to feel neglected.

Love Tastes Divine

Love is an ingredient that goes well with just about anything: the more love you put into something, the more desirable and pleasing it becomes. Love is food for the heart and nourishment for the soul.

Ω

When Love Sees

They say that love is blind, but how can that be, when love sees through everything?

Ω

It Exists

Love is not a feeling. It is a fact of life. Whether you believe in its power or not, it exists and cannot be denied.

Ω

A global understanding: A love softly spoken is clearly understood by all.

A Wheel in Motion

Love, in some ways, is like a resilient wheel in motion; but it still requires proper maintenance in order to withstand the unforeseen obstacles that lie hidden in its path.

Ω

The Giving of Oneself

Love is the giving of oneself with vigorous devotion to others. It is simply sharing with others all the inherent love you possess.

Daring to Love

To know love is to know both joy and pain. To know pain is to be human, and to be human is to dare to love again despite a wounded heart.

$$\Omega$$

God's Unceasing Love

Man can fill empty spaces in the world with myriad forms of matter … build great cities where beautiful forests and gardens existed … and construct many other unusual wonders. Man can fill virtually any noticeable void in the world, though he still is not without his limitations. In the ultimate, cosmic scheme of things, only our heavenly Father's unceasing and outpouring love can truly fill the more significant voids in the existing universe, not least of all, the spiritual ones that, unfortunately, exist far closer to home in the hidden depths of our souls.

All That Matters

No expression of human love even comes close to the unwavering, eternal love of God, the most wholesome and uncompromising love of all, and, thus all that really matters in the world.

$$\Omega$$

Love in Action

Love is … loyalty to God and neighbor.

Love is … overcoming a human weakness.

Love is … valor—being brave in the face of danger.

Love is … enduring, strong to the end.

On Devotion

He who shows true obedience to a higher authority out of respect is wise, but he who is obedient out of love is faithfully devoted to the one.

Ω

Showing Appreciation

Nothing can be fully enjoyed in life without the proper understanding and expression of genuine appreciation. The sincere act of gratitude brings fullness of life and greater enjoyment.

Ω

On Bended Knees

When I kneel before the presence of the Lord in prayer, something truly special happens to me that never happens at any other place or time. For as I pour out my heart and soul to my Father in heaven, I am soon transformed into a new being, and by His tender grace and mercies, I am renewed once more … with a gleaming spirit that soars!

Ω

Evening and morning and at noon I will pray, and cry aloud, and He shall hear my voice. (Ps. 55:17)

Ω

As Indian leader Mahatma Gandhi so wisely said, "Prayer is the key of the morning and the bolt of the evening."

On Worshiping

There is a distinct difference between prayer and worship. Prayer is a private conversation with God. Worship is a day-to-day humble acknowledgement that He is supreme Lord and Master over every living thing ... while continuing to abide in His righteous word.

Ω

The True Atheist

An atheist who doesn't attack or criticize others for their religious beliefs is a true believer.

Ω

Love Takes Courage

It is a beautiful thing to be able to tell someone that you love them and to have the same words expressed back to you. However, love is more than just endearing words or a deep feeling someone shares with you. Love takes courage; it is a living sacrifice. It knows when to respond to the needs of others and when to say *no* when *no* means love. Love is complete devotion ... being willing to give your life over freely for the good of all.

Ω

Greater love has no one than this, than to lay down one's life for another. (John 15:13)

Ω

Blessed Is the Man

Blessed is the man who lives not for himself only, but gives of himself wholeheartedly to a higher cause ... to a higher calling.

Love Flows Eternally

Love is gentle … not soft, but strong. Love is a long flowing river, going on and on.

Ω

It's Worth It

Allowing yourself to love is simply allowing yourself to grow.

Ω

On Self-Control

There is a big difference between love and lust. Love is having patience and establishing trust. Love demonstrates self-control.

Ω

When dealing with people, remember you are not dealing with creatures of logic, but creatures of emotion.

—Dale Carnegie, writer and motivational speaker

Ω

Foolish Pride

Maturity is telling somebody you may not like, "I would like to be your friend." It is putting aside your foolish pride and making amends.

Ω

The more arguments you win, the fewer friends you will have.

—Author unknown

An Absolute Friend

Real friends are those who, when you have made a terrible mistake in judgment that resulted in hurt feelings, do not forever hold it against you; they continue to love you the same.

Ω

All Is Forgotten

Man forgives but never forgets. When God forgives, all is forgotten ... forever.

Ω

Unstoppable Forces

One of the most powerful forces in life, next to love, is the power of forgiveness.

Ω

Walking the Talk

I use to be an ardent reader of the *Holy Bible*, but it meant nothing until I decided to start living it, little by little, and believing in miracles.

Ω

Make it your aim to be at one in the spirit, and you will inevitably be at peace with one another. (Eph. 4:3 PHI)

Chapter Four: Faith and Wisdom

Kindness has converted more sinners than zeal, eloquence, or learning.
—Frederick W. Faber

Ω

Forewarned, Fore-armed

Man should not change what God has ordained, for the consequences can become deadly; like a child playing with a loaded gun, once the trigger is pulled, the damage is done.

Ω

Man-Made Things

Nothing man made is perfect; nothing man made is made to last. Yet, in a more positive light, I sleep much better knowing that all corruptible things made by our feeble human hands are reversible … by a greater hand from above.

A Dark Mind

The most dangerous man living among us is a stupid man with a brain.

Ω

Two Steps Forward

Sometimes it seems the more technologically advance the world gets the more uncivilized we become. I think somebody took more than one-step back. What do you think?

Ω

In Foresight

The appalling misuse of modern science and technology by shortsighted men will sadly be our undoing in the end. If we do not soon wisely adhere to the writing on the wall, the end result may one day spell out humanity's great downfall.

Ω

Forward Thinking

The most effective way of thinking outside the box is not allowing your mind to be in one.

Ω

On History

The commonly held assumption that history repeats itself could not be further from the truth, for it is not history that repeats itself. The true fault lies in reckless, stubborn men, who, in their willful arrogance, refuse to acknowledge humanity's glaring mistakes.

The sole purpose of learning from our mistakes is that we don't repeat them; otherwise we've learned nothing.

Ω

Changing Within

History is what it is. We cannot do anything to change its negative aspects. All we can change, for better or worse, is ourselves and the direction of our lives.

Ω

The Time Has Come

Mankind, show your humanity; confess your sins against Mother Earth and put a stop to them. The time has come now to heal the wounds and to restore her former beauty, if not for our sake, then for the sake of our beloved children. Let us not ever forget that the precious earth and all of its remaining wonders are rightfully theirs, too.

Ω

Being in Harmony

An uncluttered environment is an uncluttered mind. An uncluttered mind is an uncluttered world.

Ω

Preservation: It makes perfect sense that if we save our planet we save ourselves.

Main Endeavor

We have today at our disposal the technology to send human beings to the moon and back, to send unmanned space probes to visit neighboring planets, Venus and Mars, and to venture even beyond. We call this progress. Yet millions of our fellow beings still go without such necessities as proper food, shelter, and fresh drinking water, when this needn't be.

We must ask ourselves: "How does a civilized world justify this paradox?" Does it not seem strange that we could reach for distant stars when so many people here in our own world are starving for simple love and attention? I agree, technology is a marvelous wonder but, when utilized intelligently and put into its proper perspective, it can be much more … it can be glorious.

Let's put mankind first above the stars; let's put humanity above the clouds and sky, and reach out instead to one another with kindness and humility. In the pursuit of happiness and global preservation, this should be our main endeavor, before attempting to explore the vast unknown. If this isn't true progress … then hell, I don't know what is.

As psychotherapist and philosopher Nathaniel Branden said, "This earth is the distant star we must find a way to reach."

Ω

Out of the Womb

Darkness was replaced by the splendor of light, silence replaced by sound. Images of strange life preceded me from out of the womb. Suddenly, with the breath of life I cried, and my eyes opened. As time went on, my eyes opened wider … only to observe a strange world around me, and I cried again, this time … for divine deliverance.

A Bold Change

One time, while skimming through a popular newsmagazine, I came across an intriguing article that asked the question, "If you could change anything in the world, what would it be?" Without a moment's thought or hesitation, my answer was "human nature." Common sense dictates that if the world is ever going to change for the better, it will have to begin with a bold change of monumental proportion how we interact with one another—and more importantly, how we show proper respect for one another's belief systems and values. Ultimately, in the hope for long-lasting peace, human nature and its self-centered ways will have to submit to a new way of reasoning. As mature beings, we must come to accept the astute realization that the needs of others and their respective viewpoints are just as important and valid as our very own.

Ω

Where there is no vision the people perish. (Prov. 29:18 KJV)

Ω

To Make a Difference

There comes a time in a man's life when he has to make a pivotal decision on what is morally best for the majority at hand; for the betterment of mankind, he has to decide what part he is going to play. Is he going to make a positive difference, or just be a sideline spectator in the arena of life?

Ω

As civil rights leader Martin Luther King Jr. poignantly expressed, "The ultimate measure of a man is not where he stands in moments of comfort and convenience, but where he stands at times of challenge and controversy."

On the topic of personal faith, U.S. president and Nobel Peace Prize laureate Jimmy Carter expressed it perfectly when he stated the following: "I have one life and one chance to make it count for something … I'm free to choose what that something is, and the something I've chosen is my faith. Now, my faith goes beyond theology and religion and requires considerable work and effort. My faith demands—this is not optional—my faith demands that I do whatever I can, wherever I can, whenever I can, for as long as I can, with whatever I have to make a difference."

Ω

Without faith what does a man really have? Without faith he becomes soulless.

What Have I to Fear?

I have been told more than once in my life that I was walking on dangerously thin ice because of my spiritual beliefs. But I always said to myself, when I was being ridiculed for my beliefs, is that if Christ can walk on water, I have nothing to fear.

Ω

Whatever enlarges hope, will also exalt courage.

—Samual Johnson, writer

Ω

The Light of Hope

As the saying aptly goes: "Where there is life, there is hope." Even truer than this is the fact that where there is hope, there is also the definite presence of God, and where God is present, there is always light at the end and beginning of every tunnel.

Love Is

Love is the hope worth living for. Love is the faith that transcends all.

Ω

Today's Message

If we do not wake up each day with a genuine appreciation for life, then we need to adjust our nightly prayers. We need to ask God for a spirit of gratitude before material things.

Live as if everything you do will eventually be known.

—Hugh Prather, writer

Ω

Answered Prayers

All heartfelt prayers are always answered, even if the answer is *no*.

Ω

Another Reminder

If, on any day you wish to have a genuine religious experience, indeed you can, by just praising God for allowing you a new one.

Ω

The Good Fight

When feeling a bit weary in the faith and battle-worn from life's trials and tribulations, remember your higher calling and continue to do the right thing ... fighting the good fight. With God in your corner, you will have all the strength you will need to be victorious.

Rewards that Last

The saying "Good guys finish last" is sad, but often true. Though be that as it may, their eternal reward is always greater.

Ω

So the last will be first and the first last … (Matt. 20:16)

Inner Strength

If you can remain calm and silent when somebody insults you, sometimes nothing said says a lot, and you will have said far more than you realize.

Ω

Do not answer a fool according to his folly, lest you also be like him. (Prov. 26:4)

Ω

Virtue: Thinking like a man of passion; acting like a man of principle.

Ω

Actions Speak

It is indeed true: actions speak louder than words. But consistent faith speaks louder than both. Faith is spiritual action in play.

Ω

The only limit to our realization of tomorrow will be our doubts of today. Let us move forward with strong and active faith.

—Franklin D. Roosevelt, 32nd U.S. president

An unlimited resource: When you have run out of hope, turn on the faith.

Ω

What Must I Do?

How do you turn hate into love? What must I do? What can be done? When someone is trying desperately to hurt me or someone I love, how do I find love for the person who has caused me to weep bitter tears while I longed to sleep; how do I express love when there is only hate inside? Where do I go to find the remedy for this debilitating disease? Here I am, Lord, asking you now on my knees … I have found the answer.

Ω

There is no fear in love; but perfect love casts out fear, because fear involves torment. But he who fears has not been made perfect in love. (1 John 4:18)

Ω

When the World Is Unkind

When trials beset you and when the world seems unkind, don't turn to God as a last resort, instead make it a point to go to Him first.

Ω

On Spiritual Growth

Spiritual knowledge does not mean spiritual conversion; it does not make you more righteous than another. It is what you do, not what you know, that makes you grow spiritually.

I have thought much about the course of my life and always turned back to thy instruction. And, I have found more joy along the path of thy instruction than in any kind of wealth. (Ps. 119:59, 14 NEB)

Ω

Wisdom before Knowledge

If we had all the cosmic answers, life would be boring, unless we had the infinite wisdom of God to put them to good use.

Ω

At times I am obliged to agree with Emerson: "A man is a god in ruins."

Ω

The Human Mind

The power of the human mind, I believe, works best in combination and in cooperation with the spirit and mind of God. Otherwise, independent from its creator, its potential is vastly limited.

Ω

U.S. educator and renowned historian, A. Whitney Griswold, on individual creativity, expressed: "Could Hamlet have been written by a committee or the Mona Lisa painted by a club? Could the New Testament have been composed as a conference report? Creative ideas do not spring from groups. They spring from individuals. The divine spark leaps from the finger of God to the finger of Adam."

Genius does not come of man himself, but by and through God alone.

Absolute Power?

The famous saying by Lord Acton, "Absolute power corrupts absolutely," has always puzzled me; for, besides God, the ultimate ruler of the universe, who else can boldly claim, unequivocally, to hold absolute power?

Ω

The Evil Ruler

In light of these transformative times in which we live, I felt the urgent need to include this perceptive quote of unknown origin: "He who is all-powerful is free to perform both good and evil acts. And because good is harder to accomplish than evil, he would best show his power in the enactment of good. He who performs nothing but evil is enslaved to evil and does forfeit his power of choice. The evil ruler is no ruler at all."

Ω

The Ultimate Force

The father of quantum theory and Nobel Prize recipient, physicist Max Planck (1858-1947), on the existence of an unknown intelligent force, stated the following: "All matter originates and exists only by virtue of a force ... We must assume behind this force the existence of a conscious and intelligent Mind. This Mind is the matrix of all matter."

One's Faith

What is the true religion? Although I have my personal convictions, who can say for sure—it's all a matter of one's faith. However, all peaceful religions are important, especially if they inspire love and goodwill towards our fellow man and growing appreciation for our differences, instead of fears and condemnation. Religion, in its purest form, evokes in one an inner peace and wholeness that is carried over and felt throughout the world.

Ω

A Timeless Lesson

I believe the following biblical lesson from the New Testament Book of Luke is one that most of us should practice a bit more in our daily lives. Just think how many world problems and conflicts could be resolved if it were so.

Ω

Judge not, and you shall not be judged. Condemn not, and you shall not be condemned. Forgive, and you will be forgiven. (Luke 6:37)

Ω

Corrective Punishment

At times we are called on to make judgments on the actions others, however, let us not forget that, when we pass judgment on others, we must be careful not to rush into total condemnation. Total and irreversible condemnation will defeat the ultimate purpose—that is, if our true purpose is to encourage others to change their self-destructive ways.

Chapter Five: Human Nature and Miracles

We are what we think. All that we are arises with our thoughts. With our thoughts, we make our world.

—Buddha

Ω

Shaping Our Thoughts

Those who spend an inordinate amount of time in negative thoughts are living counterproductive lives. Moreover, if they do not alter this self-defeating way of thinking, they will soon find themselves in an isolated world of their own creation. On the positive side, this will never happen if one displays an upbeat attitude and a creative way of thinking.

Ω

Man's Stupidity

I cannot believe a person would hate another simply because of religion or skin color. This is just stupidity, moreover, an ugly sin.

Disparaging Words

Hateful words offend us only when we give validity to them.

Ω

The mind of a bigot is like the pupil of an eye, the more light you pour upon it, the more it will contract.

—Oliver Wendell Holmes Sr., physician

Ω

Civil rights activist Eldridge Cleaver correctly stated, "The price of hating other human beings is loving oneself less."

Ω

From the Inside First

If only people could see you from the inside first, instead of out, things would be a lot different all around.

Ω

On Discrimination

What keeps a person from advancing is not race, color, or religion; it's a defeatist attitude.

Ω

Six foibles need to be overcome in order to achieve success: drowsiness, indolence, fear, anger, slovenliness and verbosity.

—Ancient Sanskrit verse

Our Heritage

It is good to have a sense of pride in one's heritage, but it should be a respectful pride, not an arrogant one. We all know that no one gets to choose his or her own heritage. I am glad that the decision for mine was preordained, as I believe it is so for all by divine order. For this fact, I remain thankful and respectfully proud of my heritage.

$$\Omega$$

An Insight

As long as I recognize that I am a creation and child of God, it doesn't matter to me what part of the world I came from. On a spiritual level, such matters are immaterial.

$$\Omega$$

My Own Path

I will always be proud of my U. S. citizenship, and equally proud of my Latin heritage. My national citizenship and family heritage are, however, only part of who I am. They do not make me who I am nor define me as a human being, because I am also a growing, free spirit ... free to choose my own identity and direction in life ... my own special path for my soul.

$$\Omega$$

A No-Win Battle

Being stereotyped by someone who does so through ignorance or bias is disappointing. However, it is sadder when someone from your own racial background does it to project onto you his own feelings of inferiority.

I could not agree more with Danish theologian and philosopher Søren Kierkegaard when he said, "Once you label me, you negate me."

Ω

Across the Universe

We all have our unique paths in life that we must take to find ourselves, but they eventually lead us all back to the same universe.

Ω

One Race for Mankind

The only race that I am interested in and would be willing to adhere to for the rest of my life is the one that offers salvation as a prize for crossing the finish line.

Ω

My Last Words

My hope is that when I die, I will be able to say, with total conviction upon my last breath, the words of the apostle Paul in 2 Timothy 4:7–8: "I have fought the good fight, I have finished the race, I have kept the faith. Finally, there is laid up for me the crown of righteousness, which the Lord, the righteous judge, will give to me on that Day, and not to me only but also to all who have loved His appearing."

Ω

Peace Need Not Be Elusive

Why must peace be so elusive to mankind when all that needs to be done is to wholly trust in God's irrefutable laws of peace, and put into practice His principles on mutual cooperation and brotherly love?

In a sobering speech in 1984, on the point of God and country, Ronald Reagan proclaimed the following: "Without God there is no virtue because there is no prompting of the conscience ... without God there is a coarsening of the society; without God democracy will not and cannot long endure ... if we ever forget that we are one nation under God, then we will be a nation gone under."

Ω

I Think Not

I sometimes wonder what man really knows about humankind. Does man really know—apart from God's eternal truths—anything substantial? Can we, from our own wisdom, produce long-lasting happiness and achieve real peace with our neighbor without putting into effect God's infinite laws? I do not think so and I am not alone.

Ω

Our civilization cannot survive materially unless it be redeemed spiritually.

—Woodrow Wilson, 28th U.S. president

Ω

On Faith

If I were to describe *faith* by another word, it would be *obedience.* Obedience lights the eternal candle of faith.

Ω

Character is made by many acts; it may be lost by a single one.

—Author unknown

Infinitely More

Like other subjects, spiritual knowledge can be taught and learned academically, however, it means infinitely more when it is miraculously revealed, and understood spiritually, and "written on the tablet of one's own heart."

Ω

Esteemed Physicist Albert Einstein said, "There are only two ways to live your life—one is as if everything is a miracle, the other is as though nothing is a miracle."

Ω

Believing Is Seeing

One of the greatest miracles in life is the ability to recognize one, when it appears before you.

Ω

On Divine Intervention

Some people say there are no miracles in the world. They ask, "If God exists, then why doesn't He prevent bad things from happening to us?" I, like many others, do not see it this way. My faith tells me every good thing that exists in heaven and on earth is the direct result of divine planning and intervention. Unfortunately, most of the time we are too occupied with our self-important lives to notice it and give credit where it is rightfully due. Let us thank God, for all the good He does, and has done from the beginning of time, and for what is yet to be known.

Designer Miracles

Miracles do not just happen. They are intelligently planned and brought into being by an Intelligent Planner.

Ω

Counting Your Blessings

Count your blessings one by one, and after you come up with a total (as if such a thing were possible), thank God and be grateful for each and every one, for all good things come from above and are given freely in love.

Ω

Look at everything as if you were seeing it either for the first or last time. Then your time on Earth will be filled with glory.

—Author unknown

Ω

Where Would One Begin?

You can never truly count your blessings, for they are just too many. If, or when, you do decide to start counting, save yourself some time by starting at one million.

Ω

Appreciate What's There

The more you search for something or someone that your heart keeps telling you is not there, the harder you make it for yourself to appreciate every true blessing that is.

Stubbornness

Why do we insist on learning life the hard way? There's got to be a simple explanation.

Ω

Better to Give

We shouldn't live to get, but to give. If everyone lived this way, things would only get better.

Ω

On Giving

As the Good Book demonstrates in so many ways, the real blessing in life is in the act of giving, in the genuine desire of wanting to give solely for the sake of giving.

Ω

The Best Gift

Many say money is the best gift that you can give a loved one. I believe the best gift you can give is a part of yourself.

Ω

He who receives a gift doesn't measure it.

—African proverb

Time to Grow Up

It was once stated, "The man who dies with the most toys wins." My rebuttal is the man who dies with the most toys never grew up and never really made a difference worth noting.

Ω

On Self-Worth

If you allow money or possessions to define your self-worth, you will be hugely disappointed, for all the riches you acquire will never be enough to satisfy your empty soul.

Ω

For what will it profit a man if he gains the whole world, and loses his own soul? (Mark 8:36)

Ω

When money becomes the source of inspiration, it never pays off.

Ω

Best selling author Ari Kiev, MD, in his book *A Strategy for Daily Living*, writes: "Efforts motivated solely by monetary reward invariably lead only to frustration."

Ω

That man is the richest whose pleasures are the cheapest.

—Henry David Thoreau, writer

Fulfillment: Money is the reward; fulfillment is a job well done.

$$\Omega$$

On Quality

I have learned that the money we earn is worth nothing unless it is spent on good investments. When we invest in ourselves and in the future of our children, quality should be the main priority.

$$\Omega$$

Patience Is a Virtue

Why is it when ungrateful malcontents are impatiently lacking in *something* in their personal lives, what they tend to have in abundance is negative complaints? Given the chance, all I would say to them is, "Stop complaining and start changing!"

$$\Omega$$

Reconsider

Life is much too short to remain bitter over anything. Why be bitter when you can simply reconsider.

$$\Omega$$

Keeping Cheerful

A cheerful smile will cost you nothing, but a perpetual negative frown can cost you everything. It can cost you opportunities and blessings.

Waste Not, Want Not

When I came home last night and entered the living room, I said, "Let there be light," and there was light, and the light was good, because it enabled me to see my way around without stumbling. Unfortunately, the light in my home was not free. It costs money and money does not grow on magical trees. So latter, when I proceeded to an adjoining room, I turned off the wonderful light and it made my wallet very, very pleased.

Ω

Getting the Mail

When there's a letter in my mailbox, I say a short prayer, "Dear God, let it be a check; let it be good news. Please let it be something that I can use. Amen. P.S. The fewer bills I receive the fewer the ills."

Ω

Common Sense

When it comes to lending money, if you don't have it to spend, then you really don't have it to lend. In other words, if you can't afford to spend it for your own needs now, then best not to lend it. Common sense says, stay away from further debt.

Ω

Live within Your Means

A rich man is someone who can spend a lot of money and still be rich. A poor man is a man who spends a lot of money that he doesn't have.

On Contentment

To me, a rich man is a man who has learned to be content despite his economic status. Rich or broke, he remains humble.

Ω

Strength: Money is power, but love is stronger.

Ω

On Selfishness

To love is to give, and to give is to show love towards others. To endlessly aspire to get for the sake of getting is being selfish, and failing to understand the meaning of love. Without love, what we have amounts to nothing.

Ω

A World without Love

A world without love is like a planet without a sun. A world without love is a world in darkness. A world without love is inconceivable.

Ω

For You, Mom

The following piece, entitled "On Helping Others," is dedicated to my courageous mom, Elizabeth Smith, for her humanitarian work as a translator in Guatemala where she assisted an American volunteer medical team of committed surgeons, anesthesiologists and nurses who were there to perform reconstructive surgeries on Guatemalan children afflicted with birth defects known as cleft lip and cleft palate.

On another inspiring note, one of my mom's visits to Guatemala in 2000 happily resulted in the successful intervention of a small child's life from possible tragedy. Had, my mother, not firmly insisted that the local Guatemalan doctors and nuns attend to a very sick, malnourished baby girl, the child most likely would have died on the trip back home to her native country, Mexico. Thanks to my mother's quick thinking and persistence, the frail child was put into a special program where she received the proper food and medical attention.

I am proud to say that, out of the five volunteer trips my mother made to Guatemala, this was only one incident of many on which she went above and beyond the call of duty reaching out to assist those in dire need. I thank you, Mom, once again, for your inspiring example of self-sacrifice, kindness and devotion, not only to your own family and friends, but also to complete strangers near and far.

Ω

On Helping Others

What good is the accumulation of worldly possessions if we don't put them to good use by helping those in dire need, moreover, the acquisition of material wealth if we don't apply it for the goodness of all? Isn't it true that when we give, all receive?

Ω

I think I began learning long ago that those who are happiest are those who do the most for others.

—Booker T. Washington, educator

Thinking Out Loud

"The only time I care what other people are thinking is when they are thinking what I am thinking." I say this jokingly. However, instead of being so egocentric, what I press myself to think about is how I can be more useful to my community and to others less fortunate in the world. Are you thinking what I am thinking?

Ω

Unshared joy is an unlighted candle.

—Spanish proverb

Ω

Strive for success by giving your best. As Robert Louis Stevenson wrote, "That man is a success who has laughed often and loved much; who has filled his niche and loved his task; who leaves the world better than he found it; who looked for the best in others and gave the best he had."

Chapter Six: Universal Truths and Ideals

We all live with the objective of being happy; our lives are all different and yet the same.

—Anne Frank

Ω

Thoughtfulness

Good manners simply mean showing a genuine consideration for others. It is a state of character that mirrors a caring attitude for your fellow man, and, in all manner and ways, should reflect us all.

As iron sharpens iron, so one sharpens another. (Prov. 27:17 NIV)

Ω

Preventive Medicine

Like proper dieting and exercise, frequent laughter is essential for good health. Laughter is, indeed the best medicine, and the least expensive, too.

On Humor

Because a certain joke makes one laugh does not mean it is genuinely funny. The purpose of humor is to inspire each other to a higher level of being—to bring us closer to one another—not to degrade and belittle others for desperate, cheap laughs.

Ω

The Joke Is on You

A so-called harmless joke isn't really funny, unless all are happily laughing along; otherwise, it's just plain old human sarcasm trying to pass itself off for good-natured humor.

Ω

Lasting Impressions

To make a good, lasting impression, make a good first impression. It may be the only chance you get.

Ω

A Double Vice

There are two kinds of people in the world: those who smoke and those who don't. A message for those who do: "The earth is not an ashtray."

Ω

Man is a clever animal who behaves like an imbecile.

—Albert Schweitzer, philosopher

A Place for Everything

When you see a cigarette butt on the ground, you know a nonsmoker did not throw it there, which sometimes makes me wonder to myself just how much of the rest of the garbage seen along side it belongs to the thoughtless "tobacco inhaler," too.

Ω

When Not to Experiment

Don't start a bad habit for which many others desperately seek a cure. Experimentation leads to miserable addiction, and often to death.

Ω

A Choice Addiction

Bad habits begin in the mind; hence, that's where they must end, not transcend.

Ω

Way to Destruction

Lack of consideration for others is a sure way to destruction—total cooperation is a better alternative, if the objective is to achieve a safer and better world.

A Rebel

A rebel without a cause is no rebel at all, just a person hell-bent on self-destruction.

Ω

Urgent message: Stop! Think about what you're doing.

A Narrow Mind

It takes a small-minded person to say out loud to someone—with sneering contempt, "You do-gooder." Well, my answer to this person would simply be, "Thank you. Thank you for the unintentional compliment, for I would rather be known for doing small good deeds for others than to be known for being a chronic complainer."

Ω

"Rudeness," as longshoreman and philosopher Eric Hoffer once said, "is a weak man's imitation of strength."

Ω

On Destructive Criticism

When someone is overly critical of my work ethic, personal job skills, or general outlook on life, I return to an insightful lesson I learned some years ago: unjust criticism is often a disguised compliment.

Ω

Drawing the Line

I can tolerate an arrogant person, and, at times, I can even put up with an ignorant person. Yet when it comes to a person who is both arrogant and ignorant, I draw the line.

Ω

A Beautiful Mind

An intelligent man does not argue with an angry person who insists on being right. He already knows what is truly relevant: not vehemently insisting which point is right or which point is wrong, but not losing himself to pointless anger.

Stupidity: Don't answer to stupidity, let stupidity answer for itself.

Ω

Get Real

I wonder for those who, as an excuse for their actions say, "I didn't ask to be born." Does that mean they would have replied "no" had they been?

Ω

Living on the Edge

What does it mean when people say, "Let's live a little"? Are they implying that we're deadheads? Must certain reckless people feel like they're alive only if they're living dangerously on the edge? Keep in mind that those who live this way, who take foolish chances with their lives, are bound to slip off the edge eventually.

Life's Absurdities

Whoever claims they did it "my way," like in the famed song, is delusional. Whoever says they lived a life without regrets is *full of it*.

Ω

On Regrets

To say you have no regrets in life is to say that you have never hurt or offended another human being. To believe you have no regrets is to be in denial.

Ω

The minute a man is convinced he's interesting, he isn't.

—Stephen Leacock, humorist

Pedestals Are for Statues

Don't believe in your own myth, or in all the praises others bestow on you when you're on top. Remain humble and keep your feet on the ground, for the fall from grace is always harder the higher the pedestal.

Ω

Sports Logic

A sports manager decides for his team who is going to play, not who is going to play well.

Ω

It's Just a Game!

Let's not kid ourselves, unlike true heroes, sports heroes are only that, *sports* heroes. We needn't put them on grand, lofty pedestals for simply achieving on the playing field, nor scream for their heads for failing to score the winning goal.

Ω

On Knowing Others

When getting to know someone, the truth is you never really know who you know until you know what they know.

Ω

A Lifelong Process

No matter how good a student you were, higher education never ends. It is a lifelong process. We must continue to learn what we can from the "Graduate School of Life."

Education is power; wisdom is salvation.

Ω

Problem Solving

Why is it that more people tend to overreact first, instead of thinking first, when faced with a sudden problem?

Ω

The problems that exist in the world today cannot be solved by the level of thinking that created them.

—Albert Einstein, physicist

Ω

What's the Problem?

The problem in the world with people is that people beget unnecessary problems, and such problems beget strife, which in turn leads to more problems. However, in a more positive light, anyone who confronts his problems head-on, and faces up to his responsibilities in a mature, intelligent manner, will have already found the beginning to the solution, by first thinking all matters patiently through ... and not being afraid.

Ω

Deal with It

Remember, the only people without any problems are those buried in the ground. So, the alternative for us then is very clear ... deal with them.

Don't be a problem worrier, be a problem solver.

—Author unknown

Ω

The Dead Know Nothing

You cannot smell the flowers when you are dead, for the dead know nothing. You cannot plan for tomorrow when you are lying stone dead in the ground. One must live in the here-and-now because there is no tomorrow when you die. Human life is not eternal; let no man tell you otherwise.

Ω

Please Remember

If your life doesn't mean anything to you, please remember it means something to me … and I have not met you.

Ω

Life Is a Gift

Life is a gift that we should not take for granted. We should all learn to appreciate it more. Life is a gift that should be loved and cherished. Let us not waste it any more.

Ω

It Will Come to You

Believe that your life means something great even if you do not know yet what it is. Just keep on believing, and one day the truth will encompass you … like a brilliant beam of light.

One Autumn Afternoon

Friend no. 1: "What are you doing?"

Friend no. 2: "Contemplating."

Friend no. 1: "Contemplating what, suicide?"

Friend no. 2: "Quite the contrary, I am contemplating the beauty and mysteries of life as I watch the autumn leaves gently descend all around me."

Friend no. 1: "In that case, do you mind if I join you?"

Being: "To be, or not to be: that is the question." "To be" is the only solution. Being is my answer.

Ω

The Human Heart

The true heart of man is the essence of his being, not the biological organ that circulates the blood in him. It is the main life force that compels him to reach beyond the common ... his present self and his highest ideals.

Ω

A Psychological Perspective

I once read in a brief article on human psychology that conveyed that just as much as personal success is a part of the human condition, so, too, is personal failure and defeat. So, if anyone tells you that they have never failed before nor have ever experienced the agony of defeat, I perceive that they're either lying or have never truly accepted life challenges that equaled, or slightly exceeded, their true abilities—and in that itself lies their true failure.

On Failure

Having multiple failures in life does not mean you are a failure. However, giving up prematurely on pursuing your dreams and never finishing what you have started will turn you into one.

Ω

Listen before You Speak

If you know not what you speak, speak not, but always listen and seek knowledge no matter what; always maintain the desire to learn.

Ω

"The only people who achieve much," noted celebrated author C. S. Lewis, "are those who want knowledge so badly that they seek it while the conditions are still unfavorable. Favorable conditions never come."

Ω

Staying Humble

To think of yourself as the best in something is to be at your worst; to remain humble is always better. By this you will strive to achieve more, and not allow complacency to set in.

Ω

No Such Thing

When it comes to humility, there is no such thing as the best of the best. Objectively speaking, there is only good and slightly better (depending on your point of view), and each one is designed to compliment the other.

Humility

Humility is not thinking low of oneself. It is thinking respectfully of others while having a genuine respect for oneself.

Ω

A Better Mindset

One cannot have a superiority complex without having an inferiority complex. Get rid of one and you will get rid of the other.

Ω

The Mighty Ego

A reminder to all egomaniacs: the bigger the ego, the bigger the problems; the bigger the problems, the larger the worries.

Ω

False Confidence

A person who feels compelled to brag constantly to others about his accomplishments is really telling everyone that he has low self-esteem.

Ω

On Human Nature

Generally, when somebody's ego is bruised, somebody else becomes amused. Sad to say, but the fact is human nature will have it no other way.

No one can make you feel inferior without your consent.

—Eleanor Roosevelt, activist

Ω

A Bruised Ego

Sometimes a bruised ego can hurt as much as a broken heart. The good news is that it doesn't take as long to mend.

Ω

A Positive Spirit

Why waste precious time blaming others for your problems? Wallowing in self-pity is pointless, for what *positive change* can come from a spirit of negativity? To live a more enriched and satisfying life, a positive spirit must prevail in all circumstances. Nothing good ever comes from a brooding mind.

Ω

On Human Suffering

Most sufferings we face in life are potential blessings in disguise, if we take to heart the vital lessons and gain strength from them.

Ω

Out of Heartache

Out of heartache comes growth, and out of growth comes maturity. Out of love comes healing of the soul.

Take Control

Instead of tolerating an emotional stress or life problem, why not just go straight to the heart of that which takes away your peace of mind, and simply say (to each one of your problems), "Enough is enough; you control me no more. I now command you." Then take appropriate action, and remain brave.

Ω

Even Pain Has a Purpose

Pain is a daily reminder to me that life is a continuous struggle. It reminds me, no matter what kind of pain it is, that no one is exempt from it. Therefore, I just have to make the best of what life throws at me. In a way, I recognize this to be a good thing, for even pain has a purpose. My dealing with different forms of pain shows me that I have the courage to live.

Letting Pain Go

Any emotional pain or mental anguish we experience in life must eventually subside—that is, as long as one can gather up the courage from within to fully let go.

Ω

Weeping may endure for a night, but joy cometh in the morning. (Ps. 30:5)

Ω

When We Lie

A lie is a very painful thing. A lie hurts like a needle in the eye, but most of the time we cry inwardly instead. If only we could see the tears flow down our cheeks when a lie is told, a lie would never be said.

Fortunately, not only does a lie have a short memory, it has a short lifespan, too.

Ω

In so few words, this Yiddish proverb says plenty: "A half truth is a whole lie."

Ω

The Power of Truth

Once confronted by the eternal light of truth, a hurtful, damaging lie loses all of its power. It must immediately return to the shadowy, grim hell from whence it came.

Ω

A Balanced Justice

How strange that there are two separate systems of justice these days in our esteemed courts of law: one for the famous and affluent and the other for the not as well-off. Perhaps this disconnect is not so strange if you think about it. In any case, despite this seeming imbalance of justice between the different economic worlds, we can all rest assured that, come Judgment Day, when all is said and done, only one form of justice will prevail: divine justice. No longer will the innocent be blindly punished nor the undeniably guilty be allowed to walk free.

But let judgment run down as waters, and righteousness as a mighty stream. (Amos 5:24 KJV)

Ω

To Err Is Human

When a person is truly sorry, forgive him. Forgive as you would want to be forgiven. Forgiveness leads to peace of mind and harmony in the soul.

Ω

Confessions

Confessions mean nothing without true repentance. What good is being sorry without changing your ways?

Ω

When wealth is lost, nothing is lost; when health is lost, something is lost; when character is lost, all is lost.

—Billy Graham, evangelist

Ω

On Honesty

Is honesty the best policy? Does it really pay to be honest? If one answers *yes,* he must be telling the truth from his personal experience. Why else would he answer in the affirmative? If, however, one has to think long and hard about it, he is only fooling himself.

From the Heart

Speak with conviction, and people will hear you … serve with devotion, and they will *follow* you.

Ω

One of the Same

A liar is a thief's best friend; in fact they're one and the same, going hand-in-hand. (Or should I say, hand in pocket!)

Ω

On Character

A person's reputation is precious, but a person's good name and character are priceless.

Ω

Fame is vapor, popularity an accident, riches take wing. Only one thing endures and that is character.

—Abraham Lincoln, 16th U. S. president

Ω

The Heart Makes the Man

I never did believe in the saying, "Clothes make the man." They do no such thing! They either enhance his appearance or cover his outer flaws.

Simplicity is the ultimate sophistication.

—Leonardo Da Vinci, artist and inventor

Ω

The Naked Truth

If people remember you mainly for the expensive garments you wear, what does that really say about you? Do the designer clothes and accessories we put on really reveal to the world our true character ... our true souls?

Ω

Unblemished Beauty

I will never quite understand certain people's fascination with getting tattoos—marking up their unblemished bodies with strange looking colors and awkward designs. For no tattoo, no matter how colorful or how artistic it may look, can ever make the human body any more beautiful, or more sensual than it already is naturally.

Ω

Side by Side

A universal truth: "When you're beautiful on the inside it shows through on the outside." When beauty is presented in this order, inner and outer beauty exist side by side.

Ω

The Lord prefers common-looking people. That is the reason he makes so many of them.

—Abraham Lincoln

A Beautiful Soul

It was once said that "beauty is in the eye of the beholder." Although this is true in a general sense, keep in mind that physical beauty is transitory and that the only beauty that lasts is the heavenly beauty of a righteous soul.

Ω

From Within

There is nothing more endearing to a man than the natural wholesome beauty of a tenderhearted woman, whose true gracefulness and genuine beauty radiate from within.

Ω

On Feminine Beauty

In my mind's eye, a woman at her best is a woman who is natural, inwardly and outwardly, and not something put together or made-up. A woman deep down in her heart knows that real beauty is not something you can make up.

Ω

What It Takes

You have to be a beautiful person yourself to recognize a beautiful person.

Chapter Seven: The Circle of Life

The whole of life, from the moment you are born to the moment you die, is a process of learning.

—Jiddu Krishnamurti

Ω

On Growing Up

Do not be in a hurry to grow up, but do grow up before you grow too old and feeble to remember to care.

Ω

The man who views the world at 50 the same as he did at 20 has wasted 30 years of his life.

—Muhammad Ali, three-time world heavyweight champion

The most graceful dancer who ever lived, Fred Astaire, said of growing old, "Old age is like everything else. To make a success of it, you've got to start young."

Ω

Our Lives in Passing

What are we rushing for? What is the hurry? What are we looking for in life with the look of worry? Pause for a moment ... and calmly look around you. You will come to realize that in terms of infinity, our lives in passing last for only a wink of an eye.

Ω

It's not the years in your life that count; it's the life in your years.

—Abraham Lincoln

Ω

Heaven's Gate

I find that no matter who lives or dies, the world goes on spinning and the sun still shines. I just hope and pray that when my time comes, heaven's gate will make room for one more.

Ω

Fear Not

The occasional fear we have of death is just a fear of the unknown. Fortunately, our natural trepidation of the unknown is a less burdensome weight than that of the constant fear of living.

Growing Wiser

There is a big difference between getting old and growing older. Getting old simply means getting on with the business of dying, while growing older is staying open-minded—living for your hopes and dreams.

Ω

A person is not old until regrets take the place of dreams.

—John Barrymore, actor

Ω

Into the World

We come into the world with nothing and we leave the world with nothing. Does this mean that our lives spent on earth are all for nothing? I must ask every now and then, "What power holds the truth for our purpose for being, what source or spoken words can tell us what it all means?" I believe somewhere there are absolute answers. Must I search the world over to learn what is true ... or can it be that the truth I seek lies somewhere within myself?

Ω

A Thousand-fold

If you look for love as if it were a hidden treasure, you will not find it, because the harder you look, the more elusive it becomes. If you were to look in another direction, to look deeply into your heart and soul, and freely express to others the inner love it reveals, it will come back to you, assuredly ... a thousand-fold.

Don't Settle

Don't settle for a selfish love; hold out for a love that will grow. Hold out for this special kind of love, and when it comes to you don't let it go. Hold on to it as though it were a lifeline to your soul.

$$\Omega$$

On Jealousy

Jealousy is not a sign of love, but a sign of insecurity that may lead to feelings of hatred.

$$\Omega$$

Making Amends

Enough is enough! Enough unkind things were said to each other. Let's put a stop to it now before we really hurt each other. Enough is enough, let us kiss now and make up; let's make amends.

$$\Omega$$

Agree to Disagree

When you fervently debate an issue with your spouse or significant other, and when you come out on top in the argument, have you really won? Sometimes we can be right at the wrong time.

$$\Omega$$

Forgiving Wrongs

Cherish your mate with enduring love, even if he or she has wronged you in some way. During such times, be patient with them, and in their moments of weakness, remain strong, and love will prevail.

Staying in Love

It is better to love and remain in love than to fall in and out of love repeatedly. It is better to grow in love, genuine love, than to lose the power to love faithfully. There is strength and power in undying love, just as there are endless possibilities for its continual growth.

Ω

Young people fall in love; mature people grow in it.

Ω

Enduring Words

One important question to ask yourself when considering marriage is if you believe that you will be able to have meaningful conversations with this person into your twilight years? What will ultimately determine a lasting, successful marriage is the capacity to engage in loving, stimulating conversation from the heart.

Ω

Happy Morning

Husband: "Good morning."

Wife: "What's so good about it?"

Husband: "Well … the fact that it's here and you and I still have each other."

Wife: "Oh … I see. Very well then, thank you, my love … and a beautiful good morning to you, too."

Words can sometimes, in moments of grace, attain the quality of deeds.

—Elie Wisel, writer and Nobel Peace Prize laureate

The Good Times

Sometimes when I'm feeling a bit lonely or blue, I remind myself of a little song I wrote a long time ago. It goes like this: "If you're feeling sad and blue, relive a happiness you once had, for this is true, happiness is when you remember; happiness is when you never forget the good times."

Ω

Coping with Loneliness

I've learned that the only effective way of coping with loneliness is to simply avoid it altogether before it envelops you and begins to swallow you up whole.

Ω

Making Choices

Too many people in the world are lonely. I refuse to be one of them. Loneliness is not a constant; it's a personal choice.

Ω

When Feeling Frustrated

When I am feeling frustrated, I think of people that I admire and places I long to be. I think of the future—a better future of undiscovered dreams. I am confident I will find my way there.

Ω

Nothing splendid has ever been achieved except by those who dared believe that something inside them was superior to circumstances.

—Bruce Fairchild Barton, writer

Keep on Pitching

Whenever I have had strong doubts about becoming a published author, I would remember what the great baseball Hall of Famer Satchel Paige said, "Never let the odds keep you from pursuing what you know in your heart you were meant to do."

Ω

Free Yourself

Free yourself from an imaginary bond that really has no hold on you; let the chains of self-doubt break away and no longer restrain you. Be the master of your own mind.

Ω

Writer Francis R. Havergal once said: "Doubt indulged soon becomes doubt realized."

Ω

Mind over Matter

After struggling with my weight for some years now, dieting for me is no longer about denying myself one of life's small pleasures (eating); instead, it is about disciplining myself towards healthful living. It is all a matter of perspective, and, yes, "mind over platter."

Ω

On Self-Esteem

Self-esteem is like a well-defined human muscle: it has to be developed over time. If you wish to obtain it and maintain it, get out there and start pumping some mental iron!

On Human Freedom

There are many things in life that man takes for granted. One is freedom. Despite the fact that our nation has long been liberated from the bondage of slavery (It is hard to imagine that it still exists in some parts of the world.), we are all slaves to our human weaknesses and personal shortcomings. Just because we have certain civil liberties does not mean we are entirely free. The beginning of real freedom is the acknowledgement that humanity has far more to learn about itself to improve the human condition.

Ω

There is no freedom for the mind that is closed to new understandings.

Ω

Assured Happiness

Exhibiting good morals is a prerequisite to all happiness. Without moral character, there can be no true happiness.

Ω

On Childish Greed

The more riches and material things people horde in life, the seemingly emptier and progressively sadder they become. Whoever believes greed is inherently a good thing is just plain deceived.

Ω

Avarice: There should be no cause for human greed in a world of plenty.

A Sound Strategy

To break the stranglehold of incessant greed within your soul, exercise human generosity, on a consistent basis, and the reward of lasting contentment will be yours.

Ω

In a Word

According to *Merriam Webster's Collegiate Dictionary*, 11th Edition, the word "cupidity" is defined as inordinate desire for wealth …. However, the more I really think about it, cupidity is just another word for stupidity, spelled with a C.

By permission. From *Merriam-Webster's Collegiate® Dictionary, 11th Edition* ©2008 by Merriam-Webster, Incorporated (www.Merriam-Webster.com).

Ω

Counting the Cost

There is nothing wrong with a desire to be financially wealthy, as long as one doesn't become obsessed with it to the point where nothing else matters, including family, friends, health, and, not least of all, peace of mind.

Ω

Planning

Make a list of the things you want in life, and then make a list of the things that you believe you already deserve, and then compare the two lists. Now get busy!

Needless Things

We all want what the other person has. To attain such things, we often go to great extremes. I find that, however, when we finally get hold of needless things, the satisfaction of "obtaining" doesn't compare to the strong desire of "wanting." The feeling of elation is transitory.

Ω

A Fact of Life

Novelties don't last, that's why they're called novelties.

Ω

The True Road to Success

A successful business venture begins at home. If you cannot properly manage your family priorities, then what good is a fortune to you along life's bittersweet road?

Ω

Retired automotive executive Lee Iacocca said: "No matter what you've done for yourself or for humanity, if you can't look back on having given love and attention to your own family, what have you really accomplished?"

Ω

You should not confuse your career with your life.

—Dave Barry, humorist

Love Is a Necessity

Love is a necessity no home should be without. It is more precious than any acquired luxury. Without love, a home is incomplete.

$$\Omega$$

A Simple Truth

Without a loving, nurturing home environment, a grand mansion or even a modest abode may just as well be a broken old shack for those residing within its fading walls.

$$\Omega$$

Home wasn't built in a day.

—Jane Ace, comedian

$$\Omega$$

On Loving Children

Never give your children what they want, give them only what they deserve. But do give them all the love you've got. In return, they will give you the world.

$$\Omega$$

When a Child Speaks

When your children speak, listen. Listen attentively to what they have to say, for just by listening you will turn one child's ordinary day into a magical one, to be warmly remembered forever and always.

Setting the Example

Remember, what you do in front of your child, could one day be what your child will do in front of you. So be the good things you want your child to be in life. Is that so hard to do?

Ω

Writer Clarence Budington Kelland said: "My father did not tell me how to live. He lived, and let me watch him do it."

Ω

The True Mistake

No child born into the world (in or out of wedlock) should ever be labeled *a mistake*. The mistake is in not giving a child the proper love and nurturing that he or she rightfully deserves. Besides, God doesn't make living mistakes, nor any other kind for that matter.

Ω

Before I formed you in the womb I knew you; before you were born I sanctified you. (Jer. 1:5)

Ω

Meant to Be

The stigma associated with being an unplanned child is unfortunate. The so-called "mistake" was in the accidental pregnancy, not in the birth. Do not ever let anyone make you feel that you are not supposed to be here.

If there is light in the soul, there will be beauty in the person. If there is beauty in the person, there will be harmony in the house. If there is harmony in the house, there will be order in the nation. If there is order in the nation, there will be peace in the world.

—Chinese proverb

Ω

On Society

In addition to steel beams, conjoining glass, and concrete, a great society must be built on a foundation of unceasing and unconditional love.

Ω

"What do we live for," as Mary Ann Evans writing as George Eliot expressed, "if it is not to make life less difficult for each other?"

Ω

Human Dignity

What do we truly live for if not to express to one another compassion and human dignity?

Ω

Courage is the price that life exacts for granting peace.

—Amelia Earhart, aviator

War of the Worlds

Why is it that our governments around the world start the problems and wars with each other and then impose upon their peaceful and younger citizens to fight for them? Like most people, I hate war; I always have; it scares the hell out of me.

$$\Omega$$

"The best government," the German writer Johann Wolfgang Von Goethe observed, is "that which teaches us to govern ourselves."

$$\Omega$$

United We Stand

A global message to all free-world leaders and politicians: An adversarial government is ultimately doomed to fail.

$$\Omega$$

Justice is the ligament which holds civilized beings and civilized nations together.

—Daniel Webster, statesman

$$\Omega$$

A Last Resort

Unfortunately there are times when war becomes wholly necessary, when war must be waged to preserve humankind from the tyrannical hands of madmen and the criminally insane.

Renowned statesman Edmund Burke summed it up best: "The only thing necessary for the triumph of evil is for good men to do nothing."

Ω

The Cost of Freedom

Never in the history of human civilization did freedom come to exist without the high price of blood and sacrifice.

Ω

In his second inaugural address, forty-third President George W. Bush expressed the following words on freedom: "There is only one force of history that can break the reign of hatred and resentment, and expose the pretensions of tyrants and reward the hopes of the decent and tolerant, and that is the force of human freedom."

Ω

True Victory

Victory is assured to all nations that strive for peace without unleashing the dogs of war.

Ω

A Call to Peace

Let's strive for peace without bloodshed. Let's work for peace with mutual respect.

No tree has branches so foolish as to fight among themselves.

—Native American proverb

Ω

Who Profits?

Apart from munitions suppliers and undertakers, who truly profits from war?

Ω

Peace is not the way. Love is the way; peace is the outcome.

Ω

Tug of War

Life is a tug of war. It is always love and hate going hand-in-hand, constantly in a tug of war with man. But one day our problems will cease, when we all come to band as one … and learn to play in unity the instruments of peace.

Ω

Looking Upward

On one day when I was a young boy, my father noticed that I was despondent over a certain matter. In an effort to lift my spirits, he said something to me along these lines: "Son, never keep your head down and never frown, always look upward and smile. If you can do this for one whole day … you could rule the world tomorrow."

A Noble Leader

A gifted leader is one who has the ability to bring out true leadership qualities in others. He instills confidence in others by gaining their absolute trust, showing that he completely supports their interests, ambitions, and dreams.

$$\Omega$$

Path to Destiny

To be an obedient follower of the virtuous path is to be the leader of your destiny.

$$\Omega$$

Leadership is action, not position.

—Author unknown

Leadership

L Loyalty.

Be trustworthy; instill confidence in others by honoring your word.

E Excellence.

Aspire to excellence in all your endeavors and goals.

A Acknowledgement.

Acknowledge your weaknesses and limitations. But do not allow them to impede you from moving forward or from trying again.

D Determination.

Remain determined to find your own path in the world while establishing a respectable name.

E Enthusiasm.

Evoke in others a passion for life and wholesome living. Like laughter, enthusiasm is contagious.

R Refinement.

Continue to refine your social and interpersonal skills. They will take you far in life.

S Sacrifice.

To ensure success, wise sacrifices must be made; life is full of trade-offs.

H Humility.

Be humble. Humility is an essential component of great leadership. A humble heart finds favor with God.

I Illumination.

Be a positive light to others: lead by example, not by lofty words.

P Perfection.

Strive for perfection, for as it is written in Matthew 5:48, "You shall be perfect, just as your Father in heaven is perfect."

My Grandmother, the True Poet

My *abuela* (grandmother), Celia López, was born in the beautiful Caribbean in 1913 on the mountainous, island jewel of Puerto Rico. She was the proud mother of four children and was an inspirational wordsmith. In 1945, after the war she, my father (who was about four years old at the time), and his younger brother Hector moved to the United States from Puerto Rico, eventually to be followed by my father's two older siblings, my endearing aunts Anna and Juanita. As my father recounts, they embarked on an old passenger ship from San Juan to New York to reunite with my grandfather, Juan López Montalvo, who was living in Brooklyn, home of the beloved Brooklyn Dodgers.

When I was about seven years old and my parents were just about into their ninth year of marriage, my grandmother came to live with us—and my little sister, Kim, for a period of about two and a half years. It was then that I discovered my grandmother's love of writing, particularly inspirational poetry and plays. As I recall, when Abuela was not writing in her journals, she was busy reciting her poetry and rehearsing her various plays (in her native Spanish) to an invisible audience. She would later perform her creative works before real spectators, in small community theater workshops, to grateful applause.

My grandmother, who was adored by many, especially for her joyous laughter and playful, tenderhearted nature, was a positive influence on me. By example, she inspired me to explore my hidden talents, and to experience the joys of creative writing and self-expression. I want to share with you a bit of her life-story. The following is a special poem written by my late, beloved grandmother, Celia López, and is based on her grateful admiration for her adopted home, the United States of America. It is entitled, "America, Beautiful Land."

America, Beautiful Land

America, beautiful land,
Land of liberty, secret of happiness,
Pilgrim's refuge.

America, you are like a beautiful golden
Sunrise that shines on us all.

America, country of liberty, secret of happiness,
In your land men have been born full of
Light, seeking equality for all.

America, you are like a tree which extends its
Branches to the birds so that they may hang
Their nest.

America, beautiful land, country of liberty,
Secret of happiness, your sweet name floats
Through the air, through the oceans, and throughout
All nations, giving inspiration to all.

America, my beloved country, land of liberty,
Secret of happiness, thank you for your inspired wisdom
And for showing us the way to true equality and freedom.

May God continue to protect and preserve our beautiful America.

—Celia López (1913-2002) writer and poet

America, Hermosa Tierra (original version)

América, tierra querida, patria de la libertad,
Secreto de felicidad, dulce nombre,
Refugio peregrino.

América, secreto de felicidad, influyéndonos a
Todos, amarnos por igual.

Tu eres como el plateado sol cuando sale nos
Alumbra a todos por igual.
En ti han nacido hombres llenos de luz,
Buscando el bien para todos igual.
Eres como el árbol que da la rama al pájaro
Para colgar su nido.

América, tu nombre va flotando por los aires,
Va flotando sobre las aguas de los inmensos
Mares y por todas las naciones, también va
Flotando en inspiración, tu dulce nombre.

América, tierra querida patria de libertad,
Secreto de felicidad, influyéndonos a todos
En el bello arte de aprender a amar,
En comprensión, sabiduría e inspiración
Por igual a todos.

Dios salve, América!

—Celia López (1913-2002) writer and poet

Brave New World

One day I would hope to see a world where it can be truly said, without contradiction, that race, color, religion, size, and form make no difference at all in our society. What truly matters is the unceasing spirit of universal brotherhood, camaraderie and eternal friendship. The sooner we start planning and building this brave new world, the sooner it will come to fruition.

Ω

A Special Journey

If successful, a special journey in life brings us full circle, allowing us to reflect on its many lessons with renewed hope and optimism… instilling in us a new sense of purpose, as we bravely move on to our next inspiring journey.

Ω

It is never too late to be what you might have been.

—George Eliot, writer

Closing Thoughts

The core message of *Matters of the Heart & Soul* is best summed up in the timeless words of the great philosopher Socrates: "Living well and beautifully and justly are all one thing." It is my hope that, after reading this book, you will be strongly motivated to reach for the best in life—to never settle for less, and become the dynamic, self-confident person you aspire to be. I thank you for being a special part of my personal journey, one I will continue to pursue, seeking new horizons, especially from within. I am grateful to you for granting me the honor of sharing with you my innermost thoughts, hopes and dreams.

About the Author

John J. Montalvo is a proud native New Yorker of Puerto Rican descent, who speaks from his inner being a positive message on the human experience. As a graduate of Fiorello H. LaGuardia Community College, he has worked in the physical rehabilitation field in New York State for over fourteen years. Throughout his tenure as a physical therapist assistant, he has administered physical therapy services in a wide range of healthcare settings, including hospital centers, nursing homes, and private sports clinics. He has also provided homecare physical therapy services for the elderly and the permanently disabled. As a firm believer in the importance of self-improvement and goal-setting, John continues to dedicate himself to his work in physical rehabilitation and to his first love of writing—aspiring to assist others with his specialized skills and encouraging insights to reach for greater heights.

Contact Information

If you would like to share your thoughts with John about the book *Matters of the Heart & Soul*, you can e-mail him at johnmontalvo501@ yahoo.com. Any feedback will be appreciated.